THE POWER OF

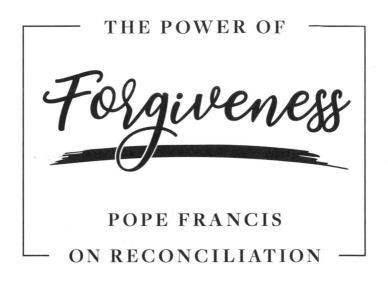

Forgiveness

POPE FRANCIS
ON RECONCILIATION

UNITED STATES CONFERENCE OF CATHOLIC BISHOPS

WASHINGTON, DC

ISBN 978-1-60137-683-1

First Printing, July 2021

Contents

Forgiveness

Foreword

There was once a teenage son who got into a horrible fight with his father. The fight was so bad that they yelled at one another. In fact, the father threw his son out of the house and told him never to come back. Ever. The teenage son yelled back he would never come back. The door slammed, and the son walked off into the crowded street of the busy city.

Several days went by, and the son wondered. Why did the argument with his father escalate so badly? What was it even about? It began with a disagreement and then worsened. He remembered the intensity, the hostility, and the bitterness. And the yelling. He wondered why he yelled. The son wished he could take it all back. But he was sure there was no way forward, or, in this case, no way back. He and his father had said too many hurtful things to each other.

The son was rather sure that his father would not take him back. Nonetheless, he decided to see. Yet he did not want to go see his father, to knock on the door. He also did not want to call on the phone. For one thing, he was too embarrassed to show up on the doorstep or have his name on the caller ID. For another, things could easily escalate again, and that would hurt too much.

So the son decided to write a note to his father that simply said, "I am sorry. If you want me to come home, please hang a large white handkerchief on the tree outside our house on Tuesday of next week. I will take the city bus that rides by the house. If the white cloth is there, I will know it is okay to come home. If the white cloth is not there, I will keep going and you won't see me again." The son mailed the letter to his father.

On Tuesday of the following week, the son boarded the bus that would go past his father's house. He was careful to take a seat by the window on the side of the bus that would pass directly in front of his dad's house. That way the son would have a clear view of the tree in the front yard.

The bus continued its run, passing block after block. It meandered and motored through its usual stops. Passengers shuffled on and off. Eventually, the father's house was two blocks away. The son got nervous. Butterflies filled his stomach. The bus turned the corner, and his father's house began to come into view.

As it did, the son closed his eyes and uttered a short prayer. He waited a moment and opened his eyes. The bus was nearly in front of his dad's house. The front yard drew close. There was the large tree. The son glimpsed up and looked. There was not one white cloth in the tree. There were *hundreds*. White cloths were tied along every branch and hung along each tree limb. A large white cloth was wrapped around the trunk. They were long and flowing and blowing in the breeze.

Statistics tell us that a lot of Catholics do not go to confession. But a lot of people sure want to be reconciled. They want the past to heal. There is an old wound somewhere in your life, isn't there? It is the place where you just walked away, or someone walked away from you. You probably do not talk about it with your friends. You do not post it out there on social media. You might not even talk about it with God. It is the two sisters who unfriended each other on Facebook a decade ago and have not spoken since. It is the two friends who had the falling out, blamed one another, and went their separate ways. Or maybe it is God himself whom you or I are angry at. There was something that God should not have allowed, and yet He did.

What keeps the old grudge alive? Is it more alive in our life than joy? Many people secretly wish the past were different. They wish that they had avoided the cliff in the relationship, they wish that they had not dug their heels in and stood by the silly ultimatum, or they wish that they had not uttered that painful phrase years ago that they now would take back if they could. Wishes hurt. Well, you do not have to wish anymore. Mercy is the opposite of wishing. Hope is the opposite of revenge. In fact, grudges are to revenge what hope is to mercy. The only way to change the past is here in the present: to live the present with forgiveness. More than anything else, that is the message of this book, *The Power of Forgiveness: Pope Francis on Reconciliation.*

Forgiveness costs, but the richest CEO in America cannot buy it. Reconciliation is not a "do-it- yourself" reality. There is nothing easy about mercy. Our path to forgiving one another does not begin with us. It *begins in* and *comes from* God. And we meet that grace of forgiveness, mercy, when we go to Confession, when we receive the Sacrament of Penance. It can be a bit intimidating to walk into the confessional or to kneel in a reconciliation room and tell our sins to a priest. But God is a loving Father who longs to forgive us. Confession, the Sacrament of Penance, is how we write that short note to God as the son did in the story above. It is how we go to our father's house and find the abundant, eager God waiting for us, to welcome us and heal us.

This book collects key points from the teaching of Pope Francis on forgiveness and presents them to us in one place for reflection. In the gentle style of Pope Francis, this easy-to-use book reminds us of our need for reconciliation, how to form our conscience, and how to prepare to "go to Confession." This book helps us on the path to forgiving one another by helping us go to God first and receiving the reconciliation that we can then share. The pages you are now holding can be read at your own pace. You hold in your hands now a trustworthy guide to help you express the desire for reconciliation and to open your heart to be renewed in God's grace.

Forgiveness changes things. Reconciliation is within reach. Write the note. Step onto the bus. Offer the short prayer, and glimpse the beautiful love of God waiting within these pages. These pages lead us to the house of the Father, to the Sacrament of Penance and the abundant mercy of God.

—Rev. Msgr. J. Brian Bransfield, STD

One

Our Need for Repentance

Pope Francis frequently reminds us of this universal truth: we are all sinners. As St. Paul tells us, "All have sinned and are deprived of the glory of God" (Rom 3:23). This is part of the human condition, an effect of Original Sin, that all humankind is vulnerable to the temptations of the Devil. The *Catechism of the Catholic Church* explains this by saying,

> *the new life received in Christian initiation has not abolished the frailty and weakness of human nature, nor the inclination to sin that tradition calls concupiscence, which remains in the baptized such that with the help of the grace of Christ they may prove themselves in the struggle of Christian life. This is the struggle of conversion directed toward holiness and eternal life to which the Lord never ceases to call us.* (no. 1426)

God extends his grace and forgiveness as his free gift to us. But as we are rational creatures endowed with free will, these gifts are not thrust upon us. Rather, we must freely respond to grace by repenting of our sins in order to accept this great gift of God's mercy. The Sacrament of Reconciliation, or confession, is the ordinary means by which our sins are forgiven under the New Covenant instituted by Christ.

Our wounded humanity

Our humanity is wounded; we know how to distinguish between good and evil, we know what is evil, we try to follow the path of goodness, but we often fall because of our weaknesses and choose evil. This is the consequence of original sin, which we are fully aware of thanks to the Book of Revelation.

The Name of God Is Mercy
Random House (2016), p. 42, Kindle Edition

Not by our efforts alone

By our efforts alone, we cannot be reconciled to God. Sin truly is the expression of the rejection of his love, with the consequence of closing in on ourselves, deluding ourselves into thinking that we have found greater freedom and autonomy. Far from God we no longer have a destination, and we are transformed from pilgrims in this world to "wanderers." To use a common expression: when we sin, we "turn away from God." That's just what we do; the sinner sees only himself and presumes in this way to be self-sufficient. Thus, sin continues to expand the distance between us and God, and this can become a chasm. However, Jesus comes to find us like a good shepherd who is not content until he has found the lost sheep, as we read in the Gospel (cf. Lk 15:4-6). He rebuilds the bridge that connects us to the Father and allows us to rediscover our dignity as children. By the offering of his life, he has reconciled us to the Father and given us eternal life (cf. Jn 10:15).

Jubilee Audience
April 30, 2016

Open up to the Word

In order to convert, we must not wait for prodigious events, but open our heart to the Word of God, which calls us to love God and neighbor. The Word of God may revive a withered heart and cure it of its blindness.

General Audience
May 18, 2016

I am weak, he is strong

Let us never tire of feeling in need of his forgiveness. For when we are weak, being close to him strengthens us and enables us to live the faith with greater joy.

Jubilee Audience
January 30, 2016

Straying from the path

This makes us understand how many times we ourselves have started out on the path of following Jesus, with the values of the Gospel, and then halfway down the road we get another idea, we see some sign or other, and we stray and conform to something more temporal, more material, more worldly—let's say—and we lose the memory of that first enthusiasm we had when we heard Jesus speak. The Lord always makes us return to that first encounter, the first moment when He looked at us, He spoke to us and He inspired in us the desire to follow Him.

This is a grace to ask of the Lord, because in life we will always have this temptation to stray because we see something else: "But that will go really well, but that's a good idea," and we distance ourselves. The grace to return to the first call, the first moment: to not forget, to not forget my history, when Jesus looked at me with love and said to me, "This is your path"; when Jesus, through many people, made me understand what the path of the Gospel is, and not other paths that are more worldly, with other values. To return to the first encounter.

Morning Meditation
April 27, 2020

How did I fall?

And all of us, when we are conquered by temptation, we end up feeling calm, because we have found a justification for this sin, for this sinful attitude, for this life which is against God's law. We should have the custom of identifying this process within us. That process that changes our hearts from good to bad, that leads us to a downward slope. A thing that grows, grows, grows slowly, then it infects others, in the end it justifies itself. It is rare that temptations come all at once, the devil is astute. And he knows how to take this path, the same one he took to arrive at Jesus' condemnation.

When we recognize that we are in sin or that we have fallen, yes, we must go and ask the Lord for forgiveness, this is the first step that we must take. But then we must say: "How did I fall into this? How did this process begin in my soul? How did it grow? Whom have I infected? And in the end how did I justify myself in order to fall?"

The life of Jesus is always an example for us. The things that happened to Jesus are things that also will happen to us: the temptations, the justifications, good people around us--and perhaps we do not listen to them--and bad people in the moment of temptation. We surround ourselves with them in order to allow the temptation to get stronger. But let us never forget: always, behind a sin, behind a fall, there is a temptation that began small, that grew, that infected us, and in the end, we find a justification to fall. May the Holy Spirit enlighten us in this interior awareness.

Morning Meditation
April 4, 2020

Where we must begin

How many times do we feel alone, that we have lost our way in life? How many times do we no longer know how to begin again, overwhelmed by the effort to accept ourselves? We need to start over, but we don't know where to begin.

Christians are born from the forgiveness they receive in Baptism. They are always reborn from the same place: from the surprising forgiveness of God, from his mercy which restores us. Only by being forgiven can we set out again with fresh confidence, after having experienced the joy of being loved by the Father to the full.

Homily, Penitential Celebration
March 29, 2019

What must I do?

Today, let us each think: what must I do before this mercy of God who awaits me and who always forgives? What must I do? We can have great trust in God's mercy but without abusing it. We must not justify spiritual laziness, but increase our commitment to respond promptly to this mercy with heartfelt sincerity.

Angelus
March 24, 2019

Recognizing that we walk darkness

Walking in darkness means being overly pleased with ourselves, believing that we do not need salvation. That is darkness! When we continue on this road of darkness, it is not easy to turn back. . . . Look to your sins, to our sins, we are all sinners, all of us . . . This is the starting point. But if we confess our sins, He is faithful, He is so just He forgives us our sins, cleansing us from all unrighteousness...The Lord who is so good, so faithful, so just that He forgives.

Morning Meditation
April 29, 2013

How to be saved?

How do I want to be saved? My way? According to a spirituality that is good, that is good for me, but that is set, having everything defined and no risks? Or in a divine manner, that is, on the path of Jesus, who always surprises us, who always opens the doors for us to that mystery of the almighty power of God, which is mercy and forgiveness?

Morning Meditation
October 3, 2014

While we were yet sinners

Think of the gossip after the call of Matthew: he associates with sinners! (cf. Mk 2:16). He comes for us when we recognize that we are sinners. But if we are like the Pharisee, before the altar, who said: I thank you Lord, that I am not like other men, and especially not like the one at the door, like that publican (cf. Lk 18:11-12), then we do not know the Lord's heart, and we will never have the joy of experiencing this mercy! It is not easy to entrust oneself to God's mercy, because it is an abyss beyond our comprehension. But we must!

Homily, Parish of St. Anna in the Vatican
March 17, 2013

Courage to return

This is important: the courage to trust in Jesus' mercy, to trust in his patience, to seek refuge always in the wounds of his love. Saint Bernard even states: "So what if my conscience gnaws at me for my many sins? 'Where sin has abounded, there grace has abounded all the more' (Rom 5:20)" (ibid.). Maybe someone among us here is thinking: my sin is so great, I am as far from God as the younger son in the parable, my unbelief is like that of Thomas; I don't have the courage to go back, to believe that God can welcome me and that he is waiting for me, of all people. But God is indeed waiting for you; he asks of you only the courage to go to him.

Homily, Papal Mass for the Possession
of the Chair of the Bishop of Rome
Divine Mercy Sunday
April 7, 2013

Being Christian means forgiving

As the Lord has forgiven you, so should you do. . . . If you do not know how to forgive, you are not a Christian . . . because you do not do as the Lord did. . . . If you don't forgive, you cannot receive the Lord's peace, the Lord's forgiveness.

Morning Meditation
September 10, 2015

Whenever we fall

In life we go forward tentatively, uncertainly, like a toddler who takes a few steps and falls; a few steps more and falls again, yet each time his father puts him back on his feet. The hand that always puts us back on our feet is mercy: God knows that without mercy we will remain on the ground, that in order to keep walking, we need to be put back on our feet.

You may object: "But I keep falling!" The Lord knows this, and he is always ready to raise you up. He does not want us to keep thinking about our failings; rather, he wants us to look to him. For when we fall, he sees children needing to be put back on their feet; in our failings he sees children in need of his merciful love.

Homily, Church of Santo Spirito in Sassia, Rome
April 19, 2020

True conversion

The Lord, who overcame the deceptions of the Tempter during the forty days in the desert, shows us the path we must take. May the Holy Spirit lead us on a true journey of conversion, so that we can rediscover the gift of God's word, be purified of the sin that blinds us, and serve Christ present in our brothers and sisters in need.

Message for Lent 2017

Sin of presumption

Do not say, "God's compassion is great, he'll forgive me my many sins, and so I continue doing what I want," . . . Do not delay to convert to the Lord, do not postpone it from day to day, for suddenly the wrath of the Lord will burst forth.

Morning Meditation
February 28, 2019

Make room for the Lord

All the same, evil is strong, it has a seductive power: it attracts and fascinates. Our own efforts are not enough to detach ourselves from it: we need a greater love. Without God, we cannot overcome evil. Only his love raises us up from within, only his tender love poured out into our hearts makes us free. If we want to be free from evil, we have to make room for the Lord who forgives and heals. He accomplishes this above all through the sacrament we are about to celebrate. Confession is the passage from misery to mercy; it is God's writing upon the heart.

Homily, Penitential Celebration
March 29, 2019

The purpose of trial

Where God and his paternity are rejected, life is no longer possible, existence loses its roots, everything appears depraved and annihilated. However, even this painful moment is in view of salvation. The purpose of trial is that the people may experience the bitterness of those who abandon God, and thus confront the distressing emptiness of choosing death. Suffering, the inevitable consequence of a self-destructive decision, must make sinners reflect in order for them to be open to conversion and forgiveness. This is the way of divine mercy.

General Audience
March 2, 2016

God keeps searching

In Jesus' vision there are no sheep that are definitively lost, but only sheep that must be found again. We need to understand this well: to God no one is definitively lost. Never! To the last moment, God is searching for us.

Think of the good thief; only in the eyes of Jesus no one is definitively lost.

General Audience
May 4, 2016

Always a child of God

I think of those who have made mistakes and cannot manage to envision the future, of those who hunger for mercy and forgiveness and believe they don't deserve it. . . . In any situation of life, I must not forget that I will never cease to be a child of God, to be a son of the Father who loves me and awaits my return. Even in the worst situation of life, God waits for me, God wants to embrace me, God expects me.

General Audience
May 11, 2016

God tries harder

God has never failed to offer his forgiveness to men and women: his mercy is felt from generation to generation. Often, we believe that our sins distance the Lord from us. In reality, in sinning, we may distance ourselves from him, but, seeing us in danger, he tries all the harder to find us. God never gives in to the possibility that a person could stay estranged from his love, provided, however, that he finds in him or her some sign of repentance for the evil done.

Jubilee Audience
April 30, 2016

We are all sinners

Today, all of us, sinners, perhaps great sinners or small sinners, but we are all sinners, the Lord says to all of us: "Have courage, come! You are no longer rejected, you are no longer rejected: I forgive you, I embrace you." God's mercy is like this.

General Audience
August 31, 2016

Give me your tired

How true are Jesus' words, which invite those who are tired and weary to come to Him to find rest! His arms outstretched on the cross show that no one is excluded from his love and his mercy, not even the greatest sinner: no one! We are all included in his love and in his mercy. The most immediate expression with which we feel welcomed and included in him is that of forgiveness. We all need to be forgiven by God. And we all need to encounter brothers and sisters who help us to go to Jesus, to open ourselves to the gift he has given us on the cross. Let us not hinder each other! Let us not exclude anyone! Rather, with humility and simplicity let us become instruments of the Father's inclusive mercy.

Jubilee Audience
November 12, 2016

No more delusions

"Blessed are the poor in spirit, for theirs is the kingdom of heaven" (Mt 5:3). Yes, blessed are those who stop deluding themselves into believing that they can save themselves from their own weaknesses without God's mercy which alone can heal. Only God's mercy can heal hearts.

General Audience
November 21, 2018

Excess self-importance

What can the Lord give to one whose heart is already filled with self-importance, with one's own success? Nothing, because a presumptuous person is incapable of receiving forgiveness, as he is satisfied by his presumed righteousness.

General Audience
January 3, 2018

Two

Awareness of Sin

Among the effects of original sin is that "human nature is weakened in its powers, subject to ignorance, suffering and the domination of death, and inclined to sin" (CCC, no. 418). The less we rely on God's grace in seeking to do God's will, the more we err in judgment, dull our conscience, and fall into sin. Left unchecked, our consciences can become so muted that we no longer discern good from evil well and therefore fail to recognize our sins. "Sin darkens the intellect," said St. Thomas Aquinas—or, put less elegantly into modern terms, "Sin makes you stupid." As Pope Francis reminds us, our spiritual battle requires that we emerge from the darkness and come into the light of Christ—and own up to our sinful habits and attitudes with complete honesty and humility.

The blinding power of sin

Jesus brings light. But the people, His people, rejected it. They were so accustomed to the darkness that the light blinded them, they did not know where to go . . . (cf. Jn 1:1-11). And this is the tragedy of our sin: sin blinds us and we cannot tolerate the light. Our eyes are sick. And Jesus clearly states it in the Gospel of Matthew: "If your eye is not sound, your whole body will be unsound. If your eye sees only darkness, how great is the darkness within you!" (cf. Mt 6:22-23). Darkness . . . And conversion is passing from darkness to light.

But what are the things that sicken the eyes, the eyes of faith? Our eyes are ill: what are the things that "drag them down," that blind them? *Vices*, the *worldly spirit*, *pride*. The vices that "drag you down" and also these three things—vices, pride, the worldly spirit—lead you to associate with others in order to remain secure in the darkness. We often speak of "mafias": this is it. But there are "spiritual mafias"; there are "domestic mafias," always seeking someone else so as to cover yourself and remain in darkness.

It is not easy to live in the light. The light shows many ugly things within us that we do not want to see: vices, sins . . . Let us think about our vices; let us think about our pride; let us think about our worldly spirit: These things blind us; they distance us from Jesus's light.

Morning Meditation
May 6, 2020

The open door

When a person begins to recognize the sickness in their soul, when the Holy Spirit—the Grace of God—acts within them and moves their heart toward an initial recognition of their own sins, he needs to find an open door, not a closed one. He needs to find acceptance, not judgment, prejudice, or condemnation. He needs to be helped, not pushed away or cast out. Sometimes, when Christians think like scholars of the law, their hearts extinguish that which the Holy Spirit lights up in the heart of a sinner when he stands at the threshold, when he starts to feel nostalgia for God.

The Name of God Is Mercy
Random House (2016), p. 68, Kindle Edition

The patience of God

We need to ask for the grace to recognize ourselves as sinners. The more we acknowledge that we are in need, the more shame and humility we feel, the sooner we will feel his embrace of grace. Jesus waits for us, he goes ahead of us, he extends his hand to us, he is patient with us. God is faithful.

The Name of God Is Mercy
Random House (2016), p. 85-86, Kindle Edition

Like a leaky bucket

Our sin is usually like a sieve, or a leaky bucket, from which grace quickly drains. "For my people have committed two evils: they have forsaken me, the fountain of living water, and dug out cisterns for themselves, cracked cisterns that can hold no water" (Jer 2:13). That is why the Lord had to teach Peter the need to "forgive seventy times seven." God keeps forgiving; we are the ones who grow weary of forgiving. God never tires of forgiving, even when he sees how hard it is for his grace to take root in the parched and rocky soil of our hearts.

Second Meditation, Spiritual Retreat, Jubilee for Priests
June 2, 2016

All are sinners

Dear brothers and sisters, often as Church we experience our own weakness and our limits. We all have them. We are all sinners. None of us can say: "I'm not a sinner." If someone among us feels that he is not a sinner, raise your hand. We all are. And this weakness, these limitations, these sins of ours . . . it is right that they stir great sorrow in us, especially when we set a bad example and we notice we [have become] a source of scandal. How many times have we heard in the neighborhood: "That person there is always going to Church, but he/she slanders everyone . . . ." This is not Christian, it is a bad example: it is a sin. And this is how we set a bad example: "and, in short, if this or that person is a Christian, then I shall become an atheist." Our witness is to make others understand what it means to be Christian.

General Audience
October 29, 2014

Doctor of souls

To understand this clearly: when a person is sick, he goes to the doctor; when a person feels he is a sinner he goes to the Lord.

General Audience
March 2, 2016

What humanity needs

Humanity needs mercy and compassion. Pius XII, more than half a century ago, said that the tragedy of our age was that it had lost its sense of sin, the awareness of sin. Today we add further to the tragedy by considering our illnesses, our sins, to be incurable, things that cannot be healed or forgiven. We lack the actual concrete experience of mercy.

The Name of God Is Mercy
Random House (2016), p. 16, Kindle Edition

The way of tenderness

The evil one makes us see and condemn our frailty, whereas the Spirit brings it to light with tender love. Tenderness is the best way to touch the frailty within us. Pointing fingers and judging others are frequently signs of an inability to accept our own weaknesses, our own frailty. Only tender love will save us from the snares of the accuser (cf. Rev 12:10). That is why it is so important to encounter God's mercy, especially in the Sacrament of Reconciliation, where we experience his truth and tenderness. Paradoxically, the evil one can also speak the truth to us, yet he does so only to condemn us. We know that God's truth does not condemn, but instead welcomes, embraces, sustains and forgives us.

Apostolic Letter Patris Corde
On the 150th Anniversary of the Proclamation of
St. Joseph as Patron of the Universal Church

Sinners, like Peter

We need to repeat it: sinners yes, corrupt no! Sinners, yes. Like the tax collector in the temple of God who did not even have the courage to raise his eyes toward heaven. Sinners, yes, like Peter, who recognized himself as one, weeping bitterly after betraying Jesus. Sinners, yes, the way the Church wisely helps us see ourselves at the beginning of every Mass, when we are invited to beat our chests and acknowledge our need for salvation and mercy.

The Name of God Is Mercy
Random House (2016), p. 84-85, Kindle Edition

"Second baptism"

The Sacrament of Penance or Confession is, in fact, like a "second baptism" that refers back always to the first to strengthen and renew it. In this sense, the day of our Baptism is the point of departure for this most beautiful journey, a journey towards God that lasts a lifetime, a journey of conversion that is continually sustained by the Sacrament of Penance.

Think about this: when we go to confess our weaknesses, our sins, we go to ask the pardon of Jesus, but we also go to renew our Baptism through his forgiveness. And this is beautiful, it is like celebrating the day of Baptism in every Confession. Therefore, Confession is not a matter of sitting down in a torture chamber, rather it is a celebration. Confession is for the baptized! To keep clean the white garment of our Christian dignity!

General Audience
November 13, 2013

No justifications

May the Lord teach us to understand this, this attitude to begin to pray. When we begin prayer with our justifications, with our certainties, it will not be a prayer: it will be speaking to the mirror. Instead, when we begin prayer with true reality—"I am a sinner"—it is a good step towards letting the Lord look upon us. May Jesus teach us this.

Morning Meditation
March 21, 2020

School of humility

There is no saint without a past nor a sinner without a future. It is enough to respond to the call with a humble and sincere heart. The Church is not a community of perfect people, but of disciples on a journey, who follow the Lord because they know they are sinners and in need of his pardon. Thus, Christian life is a school of humility which opens us to grace.

General Audience
April 13, 2016

Judging ourselves

As the Innocent One is about to die for us sinners, he pleads to the Father: "Father, forgive them; for they know not what they do" (Lk 23:34). It is on the Cross that Jesus presents the sin of the world to the mercy of the Father: the sin of all people, my sins, your sins, everyone's sins. There, on the Cross, he presents them to the Father. And with the sin of the world, all our sins are wiped away. Nothing and no one is left out of this sacrificial prayer of Jesus. That means that we must not be afraid of acknowledging and confessing ourselves as sinners. How many times have we said: "Well, this one is a sinner, he did this and that . . . ," we judge others. And you? Every one of us ought to ask ourselves: "Yes, he is a sinner. And me?"

General Audience
April 6, 2016

The Act of Penitence

All of us are sinners; and for this reason at the start of Mass we ask forgiveness. It is the Act of Penitence. It is not a matter of only thinking about the sins committed, but much more: it is the invitation to confess our sins before God and before the community, before our brothers and sisters, with humility and sincerity, like the tax collector at the Temple. If the Eucharist truly renders present the Paschal Mystery, meaning Christ's passing from death to life, then the first thing we have to do is recognize our own situation of death in order to rise again with him to new life. This helps us understand how important the Act of Penitence is.

General Audience
December 20, 2017

Stop making excuses

It is easy, and yet "so very difficult" to say: "I am a sinner, and I am ashamed of it before you, and I ask for your forgiveness." (*paraphrase*)

Morning Meditation
March 17, 2014

Let's talk it over

And today the Lord calls all of us sinners to dialogue with Him (cf. Is 1:10, 16-20). Because sin closes us up in ourselves, it makes us hide, or hide our truth, inside. It is what happened to Adam and Eve: after sinning they hid themselves because they were ashamed; they were naked (cf. Gen 3:8-10). And the sinner, when he or she feels shame, is then tempted to hide. And the Lord calls: "'Come now, let us talk this over, says the Lord' (Is 1:18); let us talk about your sin, let us talk about your situation. Do not be afraid."

Morning Meditation
March 10, 2020

Freedom through conscience

Jesus wants us free. And where is this freedom created? It is created in dialogue with God in the person's own conscience. If a Christian is unable to speak with God, if he cannot hear God in his own conscience, he is not free, he is not free.

This is why we must learn to listen to our conscience more. But be careful! This does not mean following my own ego, doing what interests me, what suits me, what

I like. . . . It is not this! The conscience is the interior place for listening to the truth, to goodness, for listening to God; it is the inner place of my relationship with him, the One who speaks to my heart and helps me to discern, to understand the way I must take and, once the decision is made, to go forward, to stay faithful.

Angelus
June 30, 2013

Saving Judas and Pilate

This is how God acts towards us sinners. The Lord continually offers us his pardon and helps us to accept it and to be aware of our wrongdoing so as to free us of it. For God wants not our condemnation, but our salvation. God does not want to condemn anyone! One of you might ask me: "But Father, didn't Pilate deserve condemnation? Did God want that?" No! God wanted to save Pilate as well as Judas, everyone! He, the Lord of Mercy, wants to save everyone! The difficulty is in allowing him to enter our hearts.

General Audience
February 3, 2016

Blessed humiliation

We must instead allow ourselves to be unmasked by these Commandments on desire, so they may show us our poverty, in order to lead us to a holy humiliation. Each of us can ask ourselves: which awful desires do I most often feel? Envy, greed, gossip? All these things that come to me from inside. We each can ask ourselves this and it will do us good. Man needs this blessed humiliation: by which he discovers he cannot free himself on his own, which is why he cries out to God in order to be saved.

General Audience
November 21, 2018

Toward the fullness of light

This inner purification implies recognition of the part of the heart that is under the influence of evil—"You know Father, I feel this way, I think this way, I see this way, and this is bad": recognizing the bad part, the part that is clouded by evil—in order to learn the art of always allowing ourselves to be trained and guided by the Holy Spirit. The journey from a sick heart, from a sinful heart, from a heart that cannot see things well because it is in sin, to the fullness of the light of the heart, is the work of the Holy Spirit.

General Audience
April 1, 2020

Three

The Mercy of God

The mercy of God is infinite and is freely given to us. His mercy is greater than any sin, Pope Francis tells us. He loves us unconditionally and wants to heal us and will do so if only we turn to him in repentance.

Pope Francis uses scriptural images to describe the mercy of God. Like the Good Shepherd, God seeks out his lost sheep earnestly in hopes of returning them to his fold. Like the father of the prodigal son who went astray, he waits for us, watches for us, and comes running to greet us and embrace us as we approach, pouring his forgiveness and mercy upon us even as we struggle to tell him of our sorrows. And he never disowns us: he is always our merciful Father, and we are always his beloved sons and daughters.

Such is the love and constancy of God, whom we encounter in Christ his Son through the ministry of the priest in the Sacrament of Reconciliation.

No limit to God's love

When faced with the gravity of sin, God responds with the fullness of mercy. Mercy will always be greater than any sin, and no one can place limits on the love of God who is ever ready to forgive.

Misericordiae Vultus
Bull of Indiction of the Extraordinary Jubilee
of Mercy, no. 3

His style: mercy

We are all warned: mercy to sinners is the style with which God acts and to this mercy he is absolutely faithful: nothing and no one can distract him from his saving will. God does not share our current throw-away culture; it doesn't count to God. God throws no one away; God loves everyone, looks for everyone: one by one! He doesn't know what "throwing people away" means, because he is entirely love, entirely mercy.

General Audience
May 4, 2016

A gratuitous act

Forgiveness is the most visible sign of the Father's love, which Jesus sought to reveal by his entire life. Every page of the Gospel is marked by this imperative of a love that loves to the point of forgiveness. Even at the last moment of his earthly life, as he was being nailed to the cross, Jesus spoke words of forgiveness: "Father, forgive them; for they know not what they do" (Lk 23:34). Nothing of what a repentant sinner places before God's mercy can be excluded from the embrace of his forgiveness. For this reason, none of us has the right to make forgiveness conditional. Mercy is always a gratuitous act of our heavenly Father, an unconditional and unmerited act of love.

Apostolic Letter
Misericordia et Misera, no. 2

His strong medicine

[God] does not want anyone to be lost. His mercy is infinitely greater than our sins, his medicine is infinitely stronger than our illnesses that he has to heal.

The Name of God Is Mercy
Random House (2016), p. 34, Kindle Edition

The two aspects of mercy

Mercy has two aspects. It involves giving, helping and serving others, but it also includes forgiveness and understanding. Matthew sums it up in one golden rule: "In everything, do to others as you would have them do to you" (7:12).

Apostolic Exhortation
Gaudete et Exsultate (*Rejoice and Be Glad*), no. 80

God anticipates us

Thinking back on my life and my experiences, to September 21, 1953, when God came to me and filled me with wonder, I have always said that the Lord precedes us, he anticipates us. I believe the same can be said for his divine mercy, which heals our wounds; he anticipates our need for it. God waits; he waits for us to concede him only the smallest glimmer of space so that he can enact his forgiveness and his charity within us.

The Name of God Is Mercy
Random House (2016), p. 34-35, Kindle Edition

The embrace of the Father's mercy

Dear friends, celebrating the Sacrament of Reconciliation means being enfolded in a warm embrace: it is the embrace of the Father's infinite mercy. Let us recall that beautiful, beautiful parable of the son who left his home with the money of his inheritance. He wasted all the money and then, when he had nothing left, he decided to return home, not as a son but as a servant. His heart was filled with so much guilt and shame. The surprise came when he began to speak, to ask for forgiveness, his father did not let him speak, he embraced him, he kissed him, and he began to make merry. But I am telling you: each time we go to confession, God embraces us. God rejoices! Let us go forward on this road.

General Audience
February 19, 2014

The careful and attentive Father

Precisely because there is sin in the world, precisely because our human nature is wounded by original sin, God, who delivered his Son for us, can only reveal himself as merciful. God is a careful and attentive father, ready to welcome any person who takes a step or even expresses the desire to take a step that leads home. He is there, staring out at the horizon, expecting us, waiting for us. No human sin—however serious—can prevail over or limit mercy.

The Name of God Is Mercy
Random House (2016), p. 51, Kindle Edition

He never abandons us

But God does not forget us, the Father never abandons us. He is a patient father, always waiting for us! He respects our freedom, but he remains faithful forever. And when we come back to him, he welcomes us like children into his house, for he never ceases, not for one instant, to wait for us with love. And his heart rejoices over every child who returns. He is celebrating because he is joy. God has this joy, when one of us sinners goes to him and asks his forgiveness.

Angelus
September 15, 2013

Not to condemn, but to encounter

To follow the way of the Lord, the Church is called on to pour its mercy over all those who recognize themselves as sinners, who assume responsibility for the evil they have committed, and who feel in need of forgiveness. The Church does not exist to condemn people but to bring about an encounter with the visceral love of God's mercy.

The Name of God Is Mercy
Random House (2016), p. 52, Kindle Edition

Always his children

As the father of the Gospel, God also continues to consider us his children, even when we get lost, and comes to us with tenderness when we return to him. He addresses us so kindly when we believe we are right. The errors we commit, even if bad, do not wear out the fidelity of his love. In the Sacrament of Reconciliation, we can always start out anew: He welcomes us, gives us the dignity of being his children and tells us: "Go ahead! Be at peace! Rise, go ahead!"

Angelus
March 6, 2016

"Come, son; come, daughter"

God never disowns us; we are his people. Even the worst of men, the worst of women, the worst of people are his children. This is God: he never ever disowns us! He always says: "Come, son; come, daughter." This is the love of our Father; this is the mercy of God. Having such a Father gives us hope, gives us confidence. This belonging should be lived out in trust and obedience, with the knowledge that everything is a gift that comes from the Father's love.

General Audience
March 2, 2016

Out of the abyss of evil

There are no situations we cannot get out of, we are not condemned to sink into quicksand, in which the more we move the deeper we sink. Jesus is there, his hand extended, ready to reach out to us and pull us out of the mud, out of sin, out of the abyss of evil into which we have fallen.

The Name of God Is Mercy
Random House (2016), p. 85, Kindle Edition

Return to basics

The time has come for the Church to take up the joyful call to mercy once more. It is time to return to the basics and to bear the weaknesses and struggles of our brothers and sisters. Mercy is the force that reawakens us to new life and instills in us the courage to look to the future with hope.

Misericordiae Vultus
Bull of Indiction of the Extraordinary Jubilee
of Mercy, no. 11

Enveloped by mercy

Dear brothers and sisters, let us be enveloped by the mercy of God; let us trust in his patience, which always gives us more time. Let us find the courage to return to his house, to dwell in his loving wounds, allowing ourselves to be loved by him and to encounter his mercy in the sacraments. We will feel his wonderful tenderness, we will feel his embrace, and we too will become more capable of mercy, patience, forgiveness and love.

Homily, Papal Mass for the Possession of the Chair of St. Peter
Divine Mercy Sunday
April 7, 2013

God forgives everything

Approaching the Sacrament by which we reconcile ourselves with God is equal to directly experiencing his mercy. It is finding the Father who forgives: God forgives everything. God understands us even in our limitations, and he even understands us in our contradictions. Not only this, but He tells us with his love that precisely when we recognize our sins, he is even closer, and he spurs us to look forward. He says even more: that when we recognize our sins and we ask for forgiveness, there is a celebration in Heaven. Jesus celebrates: this is his mercy: let us not be discouraged. Onward, forward with this!

General Audience
December 16, 2015

Everything is grace

Without grace we cannot take a step forward in Christian life. Everything is grace. It is not enough to accept the invitation to follow the Lord; one must be open to a journey of conversion, which changes the heart. The garment of mercy, which God offers us unceasingly, is the free gift of his love; it is precisely grace. And it demands to be welcomed with astonishment and joy: "Thank you, Lord, for having given me this gift."

Angelus
October 11, 2020

Forgive us our debt

From the time of our Baptism, God has forgiven us, releasing us from an intractable debt: original sin. But that is the first time. Then, with boundless mercy, he forgives us all our faults as soon as we show even the least sign of repentance. This is how God is: merciful.

Angelus
September 17, 2017

Something to celebrate

Then it is written that the Lord is "gracious," in the sense of having grace, he has compassion, and, in his greatness, he bends down to those who are weak and poor, ever ready to welcome, to understand, to forgive. He is like the father in the parable recounted in the Gospel of Luke (cf.

Lk 15:11-32): a father who does not withdraw in resentment at the younger son for having forsaken him, but on the contrary, he continues to await him—he begot him—and then he runs to meet him and embraces him. He does not even let him explain—as though he had covered his mouth—so great is his love and joy at having found him again. Then the father also goes to call the older son who is offended and does not want to join in the celebration, the son who always stayed home and who lived more as a servant than as a son. To him too, the father bends down, invites him to enter, tries to open his heart to love, so that no one is excluded from the celebration of mercy. Mercy is a celebration!

General Audience
January 13, 2016

Faithful shepherd

The Good Shepherd remains faithful even before the awareness of the sin of His own people: the Good Shepherd continues to be a Father even when His children distance themselves and abandon Him. He perseveres in His service as shepherd even with those who have bloodied His hands; He does not close His heart to those who have even made Him suffer.

General Audience
December 16, 2020

With the eyes and heart of God

This is why Jesus opens his arms to sinners. How many people even today persist in an ill-chosen life because they have found no one willing to look at them in a different way, with the eyes, or better, with the heart of God, that is, to look at them with hope. Jesus instead sees a possibility for resurrection even in those who have amassed many mistaken choices. Jesus is always there, with an open heart; he throws open that mercy that he has in his heart; he forgives, embraces, understands and draws near: that is how Jesus is!

General Audience
August 9, 2017

Four

Preparation for the Sacrament

Once we accept that we are sinners in need of God's mercy and forgiveness, what must we do? Preparation for the Sacrament of Reconciliation ought to begin with "an examination of conscience made in the light of the Word of God," says the *Catechism of the Catholic Church* (no. 1454). There are many helpful guides to how to do such an examination—a partial list of questions offered by Pope Francis appears among the excerpts below—and we also can meditate on the Ten Commandments, the Beatitudes, the Sermon on the Mount, and the moral and social teaching of the Church in order to arrive prayerfully at an acute awareness of our sins and their gravity with the help of the Holy Spirit. This practice is essential to a thorough confession.

For many, however, there is the matter of simply having the courage to face up to our sins and articulate them to a priest. Some are frustrated that they confess the same sins over and over again, as though confession cleanses us only to get sullied again. Some find the encounter off-putting, having had bad or even excruciating experiences in the confessional from having been questioned or scolded by the priest.

Pope Francis aims to change all that. He encourages us to keep returning to the sacrament as a source of divine strength and grace, even if we are bound to sin again. He says the confessional is not meant to be a "torture chamber" or "interrogation room," but rather a place where we are welcomed and shown God's mercy. He cautions us not to think of it as a "dry cleaner," but as a place of healing for our hearts and souls. We must not live in fear of returning "home" and approaching God's forgiving embrace.

Sacrament of healing

The Sacrament of Reconciliation is a sacrament of healing. When I go to confession, it is in order to be healed, to heal my soul, to heal my heart and to be healed of some wrongdoing.

General Audience
February 19, 2014

Going back home

[God] is capable of transforming us, He is capable of changing our hearts, but we must make the first step: to return. It is not going to God, no. It is going back home.

Morning Meditation
March 20, 2020

Not the "dry cleaners"

Confession is not a judgement nor is it like going to the dry cleaners who remove the stain of sins. It is the encounter with a Father who always forgives, forgives all, forgets the faults of the past and then even celebrates. (*paraphrase*)

Morning Meditation
January 23, 2015

Getting back up

The first thing that comes to mind is the phrase "I can't take it anymore!" You reach a point when you need to be understood, to be healed, to be made whole, forgiven. You need to get up again, to be able to resume your path.

The Name of God Is Mercy
Random House (2016), p. 31, Kindle Edition

Our story includes sin

Each one of us has our own story. Each one of us has our own sins. And if we do not remember, think about them: we will find them. Thank God if you find them, because if you do not find them, you are corrupt. Each one of us has his or her own sins. Let us look to the Lord, who does justice, but who is extremely merciful. Let us not be ashamed to be in the Church: let us be ashamed of being sinners. The Church is Mother to all. Let us thank God that we are not corrupt, that we are sinners.

Morning Meditation
March 30, 2020

Grace is stronger than sin

The celebration of mercy takes place in a very particular way in the Sacrament of Penance and Reconciliation. Here we feel the embrace of the Father, who comes forth to meet us and grant us the grace of being once more his sons and daughters. We are sinners and we bear the burden of contradiction between what we wish to do and what we do in fact (cf. Rom 7:14-21). Yet grace always precedes us and takes on the face of the mercy that effects our reconciliation and pardon. God makes us understand his great love for us precisely when we recognize that we are sinners. Grace is stronger than sin: it overcomes every possible form of resistance because love conquers all (cf. 1 Cor 13:7).

Apostolic Letter
Misericordia et Misera, no. 8

With a naked soul

There is a beautiful image in the liturgical hymn of the feast of Saint John the Baptist. It says that the people came to the Jordan to receive baptism, "naked in soul and foot": to pray with the naked soul, unembellished, without dressing up in one's own virtues. He, we read at the beginning of the Mass, forgives all sins but needs us to show Him our sins, with our nakedness. To pray in this way, exposed, with a naked soul, without covering up, without trusting even in what I have learned about the way to pray . . . To pray, you and I, face to face, with a naked soul. This is what the Lord teaches us.

Morning Meditation
March 21, 2020

No sinner excluded

Before Jesus, no sinner is excluded—no sinner is excluded! Because the healing power of God knows no infirmity that cannot be healed; and this must give us confidence and open our heart to the Lord, that he may come and heal us.

General Audience
April 13, 2016

Miseries of the heart

And when we prepare to receive the sacrament of Reconciliation, we must do what is called an "examination of conscience" and see what I have done before God: I have sinned. I recognize the sin. But this acknowledgment of sin cannot merely be an intellectual list of sins, saying "I have sinned," then I will say it to the priest and the priest will forgive me. This is not necessary; it is not the right thing to do. This would be like making a list of the things I need to do, or need to have, or that I have done badly, but which stays in the head.

A *true* confession of sins must remain in the heart. To go to confession is not just saying this list to the priest, "I did this, this, this and this . . . ," and then I go away, I am forgiven. No, it is not this. It takes a step, a further step, which is the confession of our miseries, but from the heart; that is, that the list I have made of bad things comes down to the heart.

Morning Meditation
March 9, 2020

Do it daily

Often discernment is exercised in small and apparently irrelevant things, since greatness of spirit is manifested in simple everyday realities. It involves striving untrammeled for all that is great, better and more beautiful, while at the same time being concerned for the little things, for each day's responsibilities and commitments. For this reason, I ask all Christians not to omit, in dialogue with the Lord, a sincere daily "examination of conscience." Discernment also enables us to recognize the concrete means that the Lord provides in his mysterious and loving plan, to make us move beyond mere good intentions.

Apostolic Exhortation
Gaudete et Exsultate (*Rejoice and Be Glad*), no. 179

Do I annoy?

Therefore, a first question arises spontaneously: do we ever conduct an examination of conscience in order to see if we too, at times, might be annoying to others? It's easy to point a finger against the faults and shortcomings of others, but we must learn to put ourselves in their shoes.

General Audience
November 16, 2016

Path to holiness

At this point, each one of us can make a little examination of conscience; we can do it right now, each one respond to himself, in silence: how have we responded up to now to the Lord's call to sanctity? Do I want to become a little better, a little more Christian? This is the path to holiness.

General Audience
November 19, 2014

A self-examination

Do I only turn to God only in my need?

Do I attend Mass on Sunday and holy days of obligation? Do I begin and end the day with prayer?

Have I been ashamed to say that I am a Christian?

Do I resist God's will? Do I insist that he does things my way?

Do I know how to forgive, share with, and help my neighbor?

Am I envious, hot-tempered, prejudiced?

Do I care for the poor and the sick?

Am I honest and fair with everyone, or do I foster a "throw-away culture?"

Do I observe the spousal and family morality taught in the Gospel?

Do I honor and respect my parents?

Have I rejected newly conceived life? Have I extinguished the gift of life? Or helped others do that?

Do I respect the environment?

Am I a believer who is somewhat worldly and only somewhat believing?

Do I overindulge in eating, drinking, smoking, or being entertained?

Am I overly concerned about my physical well-being and my possessions?

How do I use my time? Am I lazy?

Do I desire to be served?

Do I plot vengeance or harbor resentments?

Am I gentle and humble? A peacemaker?

Safeguard the Heart (*"Custodisci il cuore"*)
A Guide to Confession Distributed After the Angelus
February 22, 2015

Look beneath the surface

In order to confound the human heart, the devil, who is "a liar and the father of lies" (Jn 8:44), has always presented evil as good, falsehood as truth. That is why each of us is called to peer into our heart to see if we are falling prey to the lies of these false prophets. We must learn to look closely, beneath the surface, and to recognize what leaves a good and lasting mark on our hearts, because it comes from God and is truly for our benefit.

Message for Lent 2018

No false image

We must really recognize our sins, and not present ourselves with a false image.

Morning Meditation
June 14, 2013

Spirit of God, or spirit of the world?

We all face this interior battle, but if we do not understand how these two spirits work, how they act, we will be unable to move forward with the Spirit of God which helps us to understand Christ's thoughts, the meaning of Christ. . . .

It is very simple. . . . We have this great gift, which is the Spirit of God, but we are weak, we are sinners, and we also have the temptation of the spirit of the world. . . . [And] in this spiritual battle, in this war of the spirit, we must be victors like Jesus, but we must know the path to take. . . . An examination of conscience is so useful, to look back on the day in the evening and say, "Yes, I was tempted in this way today, I was victorious here, the Holy Spirit inspired me" . . .

If we do not do this, if we do not know what happens in our heart—and I don't say this, the Bible does—we are like "animals that understand nothing," that move along through instinct. . . . [But] we are not animals, we are children of God, baptized with the gift of the Holy Spirit. . . . This is why it is important to understand what happened in my heart today. May the Lord teach us to make an examination of conscience every day.

Morning Meditation
September 4, 2018

"Did I guard my heart?"

We can ask ourselves: Do I keep watch over myself? Do I guard my heart? My feelings? My thoughts? Do I guard the treasure of grace? Do I protect the Holy Spirit's presence within me? . . .

Let us ask the Lord for the grace to take these things seriously. He came to battle for our salvation, and he has conquered the devil.

Morning Meditation
October 11, 2013

Bedtime prayers

Which spirit did I follow today? The spirit of God or the spirit of the world? . . . This is to be done as a prayer, before going to bed, today, asking ourselves what kinds of feelings we had, identifying which spirit prompted us to which sentiments: the spirit of the world or the Spirit of God? . . .

If we are honest, we will often find that "today I was envious, I was greedy." . . . We all face this interior battle, but if we do not understand how these two spirits work, how they act, we will be unable to move forward with the Spirit of God which helps us to understand Christ's thoughts, the meaning of Christ.

Morning Meditation
September 4, 2018

Hidden idols

Today there are many idols and many idolaters . . . We all have an idol hidden within us. We might ask ourselves before God: "What is my hidden idol, what occupies the Lord's place in my heart?"

Morning Meditation
October 15, 2013

Lifeline of salvation

We are all sinners, but too often we fall into the temptation of hypocrisy, of believing ourselves to be better than
others and we say: "Just look at your sin . . . ." We all
need, however, to look to our own sins, our own shortcomings, our own mistakes, and to look to the Lord. This
is the lifeline of salvation: the relation between the "I" of
the sinner and the Lord. If I feel I am righteous, there is
no saving relationship.

General Audience
April 20, 2016

Begin with "Our Father"

If one feels bad because he has done bad things—he is
a sinner—when he prays the "Our Father" he is already
approaching the Lord. At times we may believe we do
not need anything, that we are enough for ourselves, and
that we live in complete self-sufficiency. This happens at
times! But sooner or later this illusion vanishes.

General Audience
December 9, 2020

Entrusted to mercy

Each time a person, performing the last examination of conscience of his life, discovers that his shortcomings far exceed his good deeds, he must not feel discouraged, but must entrust himself to God's mercy. And this gives us hope; it opens our heart!

General Audience
October 25, 2017

Five

The Role of the Confessor

After he declared the Extraordinary Jubilee of Mercy that began in late 2015, Pope Francis assembled more than 1,000 priests worldwide to serve as "Missionaries of Mercy" for the Jubilee year. They were commissioned to be the pope's special ambassadors to the world to preach about mercy and to promote participation in the Sacrament of Reconciliation, and they were given special faculties to forgive certain grave sins in certain cases otherwise reserved to the judgment of the papal office.

After the Extraordinary Jubilee of Mercy came to an end in late 2016, Pope Francis extended the commission of the Missionaries of Mercy indefinitely. "Their pastoral activity sought to emphasize that God places no obstacles in the way of those who seek him with a contrite heart, because he goes out to meet everyone like a father," the pope wrote in his apostolic letter, *Misericordia et Misera*. "I have received many testimonies of joy from those who encountered the Lord once more in the sacrament of

Confession. Let us not miss the opportunity to live our faith also as an experience of reconciliation" (no. 9).

Pope Francis frequently has spoken and written on the vital role of confessors. He has stressed their role in serving as a conduit of God's forgiveness and mercy. They must listen to penitents with compassion, encourage them in their journey, and assure them of God's undying love for them. They must remember that they too are sinners, and so must understand the frailty and need for mercy that is common to all persons. Pope Francis has said that "when I heard confessions, I always thought about myself, about my own sins, and about my need for mercy, and so I tried to forgive a great deal" (*The Name of God is Mercy*, p. 28, Kindle Edition). As he said plainly in a 2013 interview for La Civilta Cattolica and other Jesuit journals when asked to identify himself, "I am a sinner."

Penitents must be aware of the need for confession to a priest, for he represents Christ as well as the entire community, which also is affected whenever we sin, Pope Francis has said. Thus, "The Sacrament of Reconciliation must regain its central place in the Christian life," Pope Francis wrote (*Misericordia et Misera*, no. 11).

A community offense

In fact, the Christian community is the place where the Spirit is made present, who renews hearts in the love of God and makes all of the brethren one thing in Christ Jesus. That is why it is not enough to ask the Lord for forgiveness in one's own mind and heart, but why instead it is necessary humbly and trustingly to confess one's sins to a minister of the Church. In the celebration of this Sacrament, the priest represents not only God but also the whole community, who sees itself in the weakness of each of its members, who listens and is moved by his repentance, and who is reconciled with him, which cheers him up and accompanies him on the path of conversion and human and Christian growth.

One might say: I confess only to God. Yes, you can say to God "forgive me" and say your sins, but our sins are also committed against the brethren, and against the Church. That is why it is necessary to ask pardon of the Church, and of the brethren in the person of the priest.

General Audience
February 19, 2014

Guardians of the lost sheep

It is a huge responsibility to be a confessor. Confessors have before them the lost sheep that God loves so much; if we don't show them the love and mercy of God, we push them away and perhaps they will never come back. So embrace them and be compassionate, even if you can't absolve them.

The Name of God Is Mercy
Random House (2016), p. 17, Kindle Edition

In persona Christi

Jesus said to his apostles: "Whose sins you forgive are forgiven them, and whose sins you retain are retained" (John 20:19-23). Therefore, the apostles and all their successors—the bishops and their colleagues the priests—become instruments of God. They act *in persona Christi*.

The Name of God Is Mercy
Random House (2016), p. 21, Kindle Edition

Open hearts

I invite priests once more to prepare carefully for the ministry of Confession, which is a true priestly mission. I thank all of you from the heart for your ministry, and I ask you to be welcoming to all, witnesses of fatherly tenderness whatever the gravity of the sin involved, attentive in helping penitents to reflect on the wrong they have done, clear in presenting moral principles, willing to walk patiently beside the faithful on their penitential journey, far-sighted in discerning individual cases and generous in dispensing God's forgiveness.

Just as Jesus chose to remain silent in order to save the woman caught in adultery from the sentence of death, so every priest in the confessional should be open-hearted, since every penitent is a reminder that he himself is a sinner, but also a minister of mercy.

Apostolic Letter
Misericordia et Misera, no. 10

That tiny opening

As a confessor, even when I have found myself before a locked door, I have always tried to find a crack, just a tiny opening so that I can pry open that door and grant for-giveness and mercy.

The Name of God Is Mercy
Random House (2016), p. 26, Kindle Edition

Welcome, don't distance

At times, unfortunately, it can happen that a priest's con-duct, instead of drawing the penitent near, distances him or her. For example, in order to defend the integrity of the Gospel ideal he fails to see the steps that a person is taking day after day. This is not the way to nurture God's grace. Recognizing a sinner's repentance is tantamount to wel-coming him or her with arms wide open, after the example of the father in the parable who welcomes his son when he returns home (cf. Lk 15:20); it means not even letting him finish speaking. This has always struck me: the father did not need to hear his son's excuses; he embraced him.

Address to the Missionaries of Mercy
April 10, 2018

No "torture chambers"

Anyone who confesses does well to feel shame for his sins: shame is a grace we ask for; it is good, positive, because it makes us humble. But in a dialogue with a confessor, we need to be listened to, not interrogated. Then the confessor says whatever he needs to and offers advice delicately. This is what I meant when I said confessionals should never be torture chambers.

The Name of God Is Mercy
Random House (2016), p. 27, Kindle Edition

Our 'field hospital'

Priests who are—allow me to say the word—"aseptic," those "from the laboratory," all clean and tidy, do not help the Church. Today we can think of the Church as a "field hospital." Excuse me but I repeat it, because this is how I see it, how I feel it is: a "field hospital." Wounds need to be treated, so many wounds! So many wounds! There are so many people who are wounded by material problems, by scandals, also in the Church. . . . People wounded by the world's illusions. . . . We priests must be there, close to these people. Mercy first means treating the wounds.

Address to Parish Priests, Diocese of Rome
March 6, 2014

Resemble God in mercy

A priest needs to think of his own sins, to listen with tenderness, to pray to the Lord for a heart as merciful as his, and not to cast the first stone because he, too, is a sinner who needs to be forgiven. He needs to try to resemble God in all his mercy.

The Name of God Is Mercy
Random House (2016), p. 44, Kindle Edition

The Church's very credibility

Mercy is the very foundation of the Church's life. All of her pastoral activity should be caught up in the tenderness she makes present to believers; nothing in her preaching and in her witness to the world can be lacking in mercy. The Church's very credibility is seen in how she shows merciful and compassionate love.

Misericordiae Vultus
Bull of Indiction of the Extraordinary Year of Mercy, no. 10

"Apostolate of the ear"

Mostly, people are looking for someone to listen to them. Someone to grant them time, to listen to their dramas and difficulties. This is what I call the "apostolate of the ear," and it is important. Very important.

The Name of God Is Mercy
Random House (2016), p. 17, Kindle Edition

Listen with patience

I feel compelled to say to confessors: talk, listen with patience, and above all tell people that God loves them. And if the confessor cannot absolve a person, he needs to explain why, he needs to give them a blessing, even without the holy sacrament. The love of God exists even for those who are not disposed to receive it: that man, that woman, that boy, or that girl—they are all loved by God, they are sought out by God. Be tender with these people. Do not push them away.

The Name of God Is Mercy
Random House (2016), p. 17, Kindle Edition

Signs of the primacy of mercy

Let us never forget that to be confessors means to participate in the very mission of Jesus to be a concrete sign of the constancy of divine love that pardons and saves. We priests have received the gift of the Holy Spirit for the forgiveness of sins, and we are responsible for this. None of us wields power over this Sacrament; rather, we are faithful servants of God's mercy through it.

Every confessor must accept the faithful as the father in the parable of the prodigal son: a father who runs out to meet his son despite the fact that he has squandered away his inheritance. Confessors are called to embrace the repentant son who comes back home and to express the joy of having him back again. Let us never tire of also going out to the other son who stands outside, incapable of rejoicing, in order to explain to him that his judgement is severe and unjust and meaningless in light of the father's boundless mercy.

May confessors not ask useless questions, but like the father in the parable, interrupt the speech prepared ahead of time by the prodigal son, so that confessors will learn to accept the plea for help and mercy pouring from the heart of every penitent. In short, confessors are called to be a sign of the primacy of mercy always, everywhere, and in every situation, no matter what.

Misericordiae Vultus
Bull of Indiction of the Extraordinary Year of Mercy, no. 17

Treasure the faces

There is something unique about the face of every person who comes to us looking for God. Not everyone looks at us in the same way. . . . Only a Church capable of attentive concern for all those who knock on her door can speak to them of God. Unless you can treasure the faces of those who knock at your door, you will not be able to talk to them about God.

Second Meditation, Spiritual Retreat on the Occasion
of the Jubilee for Priests
June 2, 2016

The gaze of faith

When a penitent approaches us, it is important and comforting to recognize that we have before us the first fruit of the encounter that has already occurred with the love of God, who with his grace has opened his heart and made it available for conversion. Our priestly heart should perceive the miracle of a person who has encountered God and who has already experienced the power of His grace. There could be no true reconciliation if this did not begin with an encounter with God, which precedes the one with us confessors. This gaze of faith allows the experience of reconciliation to be established as an event whose origin is in God, the Shepherd who, as soon as he becomes aware that a sheep is lost, goes and searches until he has found it (cf. Lk 15:4-5).

Address to the Missionaries of Mercy
April 10, 2018

Confessor as penitent

I will never tire of insisting that confessors be authentic signs of the Father's mercy. We do not become good confessors automatically. We become good confessors when, above all, we allow ourselves to be penitents in search of his mercy.

Misericordiae Vultus
Bull of Indiction of the Extraordinary Year of Mercy, no. 17

Forgiven sinners first

For us priests, the fourth sacrament is the path of holiness, first of all when, like all sinners, we humbly kneel before the confessor and implore Divine Mercy for ourselves. Before going to the confessional, let us always remember—and this will help us a great deal—that first we are forgiven sinners, and only afterwards ministers of forgiveness.

Address to Participants at a Course Organized
by the Apostolic Penitentiary
March 29, 2019

Sacramental seal "indispensable"

Reconciliation itself is a benefit that the wisdom of the Church has always safeguarded with all her moral and legal might, with the sacramental seal. Although it is not always understood by the modern mentality, it is indispensable for the sanctity of the sacrament and for the freedom of conscience of the penitent, who must be certain, at any time, that the sacramental conversation will remain within the secrecy of the confessional, between one's conscience that opens to grace, and God, with the necessary mediation of the priest. The sacramental seal is indispensable and no human power has jurisdiction over it, nor can lay any claim to it.

Address to Participants at a Course Organized
by the Apostolic Penitentiary
March 29, 2019

Rigorists and laxists

It often happens that we priests hear our faithful telling us they have encountered a very "strict" priest in the confessional, or very "generous," i.e., a rigorist or a laxist. And this is not good. It is normal that there be differences in the style of confessors, but these differences cannot regard the essential, that is, sound moral doctrine and mercy.

Neither the laxist nor the rigorist bears witness to Jesus Christ, for neither the one nor the other takes care of the person he encounters. The rigorist washes his hands of them: in fact, he nails the person to the law, understood in a cold and rigid way; and the laxist also washes his hands of them: he is only apparently merciful, but in reality he does not take seriously the problems of that conscience, by minimizing the sin. True mercy takes the person into one's care, listens to him attentively, approaches the situation with respect and truth, and accompanies him on the journey of reconciliation.

Address to Parish Priests, Diocese of Rome
Thursday, March 6, 2014

The pope's confession

Priests and bishops too have to go to confession: we are all sinners. Even the Pope confesses every 15 days, because the Pope is also a sinner. And the confessor hears what I tell him, he counsels me and forgives me, because we are all in need of this forgiveness. Sometimes you hear someone claiming to confess directly to God . . . Yes, as I said before, God is always listening, but in the Sacrament of Reconciliation he sends a brother to bestow his pardon, the certainty of forgiveness, in the name of the Church.

General Audience
November 20, 2013

A heart at peace

The service that the priest assumes a ministry, on behalf of God, to forgive sins is very delicate and requires that his heart be at peace, that the priest have peace in his heart; that he not mistreat the faithful, but that he be gentle, benevolent and merciful; that he know how to plant hope in hearts and, above all, that he be aware that the brother or sister who approaches the Sacrament of Reconciliation seeking forgiveness does so just as many people approached Jesus to be healed. The priest who is not of this disposition of mind had better not administer this sacrament until he has addressed it. The penitent faithful have the right, all faithful have the right, to find in priests servants of the forgiveness of God.

General Audience
November 20, 2013

In place of the Father

His is precisely the heart of the father whom we want to encounter when we go to the confessional. Perhaps he will say something to help us better understand our sin, but we all go to find a father who helps us to change our lives; a father who gives us the strength to go on; a father who forgives us in the name of God. That is why being a confessor is such an important responsibility, because that son, that daughter who comes to you is only looking for a father. And you, priest in the confessional, you are there in the place of the Father who does justice with his mercy.

General Audience
February 3, 2016

With "empty hands"

Gestures of repentance and the few and brief words of the tax collector bear witness to his awareness of his own miserable condition. His prayer is essential. He acts out of humility, certain only that he is a sinner in need of mercy. If the pharisee asked for nothing because he already had everything, the tax collector can only beg for the mercy of God. And this is beautiful: to beg for the mercy of God! Presenting himself with "empty hands," with a bare heart and acknowledging himself to be a sinner, the tax collector shows us all the condition that is necessary in order to receive the Lord's forgiveness. In the end, he is the one, so despised, who becomes an icon of the true believer.

General Audience
June 1, 2016

Encounter with mercy

I want to remind priests that the confessional must not be a torture chamber but rather an encounter with the Lord's mercy which spurs us on to do our best. A small step, in the midst of great human limitations, can be more pleasing to God than a life which appears outwardly in order but moves through the day without confronting great difficulties. Everyone needs to be touched by the comfort and attraction of God's saving love, which is mysteriously at work in each person, above and beyond their faults and failings.

Apostolic Exhortation
Evangelii Gaudium (*The Joy of the Gospel*), no. 44

Confession, not an "interrogation room"

Many people would like to be reconciled to God, but they don't know how to do it, or they don't feel worthy, or they don't want to admit it, not even to themselves. The Christian community can and must foster the sincere return to God for those who feel this yearning. Especially those who carry out the "ministry of reconciliation" (2 Cor 5:18) are called to be instruments docile to the Holy Spirit, for where one has abandoned sin mercy can abound (cf. Rm 5:20). No one should be separated from God because of obstacles put there by mankind!

And—I want to underline this—that also goes for confessors. It's valid for them: please, don't put up obstacles for people who want to be reconciled to God. The confessor must be a father! He stands in the place of God the Father!

The confessor must welcome those who come to him to be reconciled to God and help them on the journey to this reconciliation that we are making. It is a very beautiful ministry: not a torture chamber or an interrogation room. No. It is the place where the Father receives, welcomes and forgives this person. Let us be reconciled to God! All of us! May this Holy Year be a positive time to rediscover our need for the tenderness and closeness of the Father, to return to him with all our heart.

Jubilee Audience
April 30, 2016

That liberating power

The Sacrament of Reconciliation must regain its central place in the Christian life. This requires priests capable of putting their lives at the service of the "ministry of reconciliation" (2 Cor 5:18), in such a way that, while no sincerely repentant sinner is prevented from drawing near to the love of the Father who awaits his return, everyone is afforded the opportunity of experiencing the liberating power of forgiveness.

Apostolic Letter
Misericordia et Misera, no. 11

Six

A Good Confession

Having first made a thorough examination of conscience, how do we then proceed to make a "good confession"?

In response to a question on what the penitent must do to make a good confession, Pope Francis advised: "He ought to reflect on the truth of his life, of what he feels and what he thinks before God. He ought to be able to look earnestly at himself and his sin. He ought to feel like a sinner, so that he can be amazed by God. In order to be filled with his gift of infinite mercy, we need to recognize our need, our emptiness, our wretchedness. We cannot be arrogant" (*The Name of God Is Mercy*, p. 43, Kindle Edition).

Traditionally, the elements of a good confession include a humble confessing of sins, true sorrow for these sins, a resolve to avoid sin in the future, absolution, and the performance of the penance prescribed by the priest. As the *Catechism of the Catholic Church* states (citing the

Council of Trent), to make a good confession means "to endure all things willingly, be contrite of heart, confess with the lips, and practice complete humility and fruitful satisfaction" (CCC, no. 1450).

It begins with a humble and contrite heart.

God will work with a small crack, even if a penitent cannot muster full sorrow. The pope spoke approvingly of a passage from Bruce Marshall's book *To Every Man a Penny* in which a sinful man who came to confession believed he could not repent because he was not sorry for his sins. When the priest asked him, "But are you sorry that you are not sorry?" the man replied in the affirmative. "It's true, that's how it is," Pope Francis said of this passage. "It's a good example of the lengths to which God goes to enter the heart of man, to find that small opening that will permit him to grant grace. He does not want anyone to be lost."

During the COVID-19 pandemic, Pope Francis reminded us that when we are unable to participate in the Sacrament of Reconciliation in a time of crisis, we can receive God's forgiveness from sin by an act of perfect contrition, which the *Catechism of the Catholic Church* defines as sorrow that "arises from a love by which God is loved above all else." Such perfect contrition "obtains forgiveness of mortal sins if it includes the firm resolution to have recourse to sacramental confession as soon as possible" (CCC, no. 1452).

The open door

Jesus came to save us by revealing the merciful face of God and drawing us to him with his loving Sacrifice. Thus, we must always remember that the Sacrament of Reconciliation is a true and proper path to holiness; it is the compelling sign that Jesus left to the Church so that the door of the Father's house would always remain open and thus, that men could always return to him.

Address to Participants at a Course Organized
by the Apostolic Penitentiary
March 29, 2019

Remembering our nothingness

Mercy exists, but if you don't want to receive it, if you don't recognize yourself as a sinner, it means you don't want to receive it, it means that you don't feel the need for it.

Sometimes it is hard to know exactly what happened. Sometimes you might feel skeptical and think it is impossible to get back on your feet again. Or maybe you prefer your wounds, the wounds of sin, and you behave like a dog, licking your wounds with your tongue. This is a narcissistic illness that makes people bitter. There is pleasure in feeling bitter, an unhealthy pleasure. If we do not begin by examining our wretchedness, if we stay lost and despair that we will never be forgiven, we end up licking our wounds, and they stay open and never heal. Instead, there is medicine, there is healing, we only need take a small step toward God, or at least express the desire to take it.

A tiny opening is enough. All we need to do is take our condition seriously. We need to remember and remind ourselves where we come from, what we are, our nothingness. It is important that we not think of ourselves as self-sufficient.

The Name of God Is Mercy
Random House (2016), p. 57-58, Kindle Edition

Children's confessions

I greatly enjoy hearing children confess because they are not abstract; they say what really happened. They make you smile. They are simple: they say what happened and they know what they did was wrong.

The Name of God Is Mercy
Random House (2016), p. 59, Kindle Edition

Justifying ourselves and pride

Let us not forget this, which the Lord teaches us: justifying oneself is arrogance, it is pride, it is exalting oneself. It is dressing oneself up as something that one is not. And the miseries remain within. The Pharisee justified himself. [Instead, he needed to] confess directly his own sins, without justifying them, without saying: "But no, I did this, but it was not my fault. . . ." The naked soul. The naked soul.

Morning Meditation
March 21, 2020

Concrete humility

We too need to be simple, concrete. Concreteness leads you to humility because humility is concrete. "We are all sinners" is something abstract. No: "I am a sinner because of this, this, and this." And this leads me to the shame of looking at Jesus and saying, "Forgive me." The true attitude of the sinner. "If we say we have no sin in us; we are deceiving ourselves and refusing to admit the truth" (1 Jn 1:8).

This vague abstract attitude is a way of saying we are not sinners. "Yeah, I lost my patience one time," but everything is "up in the air." I am not aware of the reality of my sins. "But you know, we all do these things. I am sorry, I am sorry." No. "It pains me, I won't do it again, I don't want to do it again, I don't want to think it again."

It is important that within us we name our sins. Concreteness. Because if we keep them up in the air, we end up in the dark.

Morning Meditation
April 29, 2020

Have no fear of confessing

We are all sinners, but we are all forgiven. We all have the opportunity to receive this forgiveness which is the mercy of God. Therefore, we mustn't be afraid to acknowledge that we are sinners, to confess that we are sinners, because every sin was borne by the Son on the Cross. When we confess it, repenting, entrusting ourselves to him, we can be certain of forgiveness.

General Audience
April 6, 2016

Confession in marriage

Marriage preparation should also provide couples with the names of places, people and services to which they can turn for help when problems arise. It is also important to remind them of the availability of the sacrament of Reconciliation, which allows them to bring their sins and past mistakes, and their relationship itself, before God, and to receive in turn his merciful forgiveness and healing strength.

Post-Synodal Apostolic Exhortation
Amoris Laetitia (The Joy of Love), no. 221

Grace of shame

When we have not only the recollection, the memory of the sins we have committed, but also the sense of shame, this touches God's heart and He responds with mercy. The journey that leads towards God's mercy consists of shame for the bad, for the evil things we have done. In this way, when I go to confession, I will say not only the list of sins, but also the feelings of confusion, of shame for having done this to a God so good, so merciful, so just.

Let us ask today for the grace of shame: to be ashamed of our sins.

Morning Meditation
March 9, 2020

To talk with a brother

Shame is also good, it is healthy to feel a little shame, because being ashamed is salutary. In my country when a person feels no shame, we say that he is "shameless"; a *"sinverguenza."* But shame too does good, because it makes us more humble, and the priest receives this confession with love and tenderness and forgives us on God's behalf. Also, from a human point of view, in order to unburden oneself, it is good to talk with a brother and tell the priest these things which are weighing so much on my heart. And one feels that one is unburdening oneself before God, with the Church, with his brother. Do not be afraid of Confession!

General Audience
February 19, 2014

The "unfair" gift

Only he who has been touched and caressed by the tenderness of his mercy really knows the Lord. For this reason, I have often said that the place where my encounter with the mercy of Jesus takes place is my sin. When you feel his merciful embrace, when you let yourself be embraced, when you are moved—that's when life can change, because that's when we try to respond to the immense and unexpected gift of grace, a gift that is so overabundant it may even seem "unfair" in our eyes. We stand before a God who knows our sins, our betrayals, our denials, our wretchedness. And yet he is there waiting for us, ready to give himself completely to us, to lift us up.

The Name of God Is Mercy
Random House (2016), p. 34-35, Kindle Edition

Words and gesture

The very fact that someone goes to the confessional indicates an initiation of repentance, even if it is not conscious. Without that initial impulse, the person would not be there. His being there is testimony to the desire for change. Words are important, but the gesture is explicit. And the gesture itself is important; sometimes the awkward and humble presence of a penitent who has difficulty expressing himself is worth more than another person's wordy account of their repentance.

The Name of God Is Mercy
Random House (2016), p. 35, Kindle Edition

God does not stand idle

Indeed, the Lord always answers the voice of those who cry out to him with a sincere heart. Those who feel abandoned and lonely can feel that God comes to encounter them. The Parable of the Prodigal Son recounts that "while he was yet at a distance, his father saw him and had compassion, and ran and embraced him" (Lk 15:20). And he threw his arms around his neck. God does not stand idle, awaiting the sinner: He runs to him, because the joy of seeing him return is too great, and God loves to rejoice, rejoice when He sees the sinner coming.

Address to the Missionaries of Mercy
April 10, 2018

Free gift of love

It is not enough to accept the invitation to follow the Lord; one must be open to a journey of conversion, which changes the heart. The garment of mercy, which God offers us unceasingly, is the free gift of his love; it is precisely grace. And it demands to be welcomed with astonishment and joy: "Thank you, Lord, for having given me this gift."

Angelus
October 11, 2020

Perfect contrition

I know that many of you go to confession before Easter so you can be right with God again. But many will say to me today: "But, Father, where can I find a priest, a confessor, when I can't leave the house? And I want to make peace with the Lord. I want Him to embrace me. I want my Daddy to embrace me . . . How can I do it if I can't find a priest?" Do what the *Catechism* says.

It is very clear. If you don't find a priest to go to confession, speak to God. He is your Father. Tell Him the truth: "Lord. I did this and this and this. Pardon me." Ask His forgiveness with all your heart with an Act of

Contrition, and promise Him, "afterward I will go to confession, but forgive me now." You will return to God's grace immediately. You yourself can draw near to God's forgiveness, as the *Catechism* teaches us, without having a priest at hand. Think about it: this is the moment! This is the right moment, the appropriate moment. An Act of Contrition made well. In this way our souls will become as white as snow.

Morning Meditation
March 20, 2020

Draw near to Jesus

To those of you who are in great suffering I say, Jesus is crucified for you, for us, for everyone. Allow the power of the Gospel to penetrate your heart and console you, to give you hope and the intimate certainty that no one is excluded from his forgiveness. You might ask me: "Tell me, Father, does a man who has done the worst things in his life, have the chance of being forgiven?"—"Yes! Yes: no one is excluded from the forgiveness of God. One

need only draw near to Jesus, penitently, with the desire
to be embraced by Him."

General Audience
September 28, 2016

Our fragility

Mankind's freedom comes from allowing the true God to
be the only Lord, and this allows one to accept one's fragility and reject the idols in one's heart.

We Christians turn our gaze to Christ crucified (cf.
Jn 19:37) who was weak, insulted and stripped of all his
possessions. But the face of the true God is revealed in
him, the true glory of love and not that of glittering deceit.
Isaiah says: "he was wounded by our transgressions" (Is
53:5). We were healed by the very weakness of a man who
was God, by his wounds. And through our weaknesses,
we can open up to God's salvation. Our healing comes
from the One who became poor, who welcomed failure,
who undertook to bear our insecurity until the end, in
order to fill it with love and strength. He comes to reveal
God's paternity to us. In Christ, our fragility is no longer

a curse but a place of encounter with the Father and the wellspring of a new strength from above.

General Audience
August 8, 2018

Seven

Healing and Absolution

"In my own life, I have so often seen God's merciful countenance, his patience; I have also seen so many people find the courage to enter the wounds of Jesus by saying to him: Lord, I am here, accept my poverty, hide my sin in your wounds, wash it away with your blood," Pope Francis has said. "And I have always seen that God did just this—he accepted them, consoled them, cleansed them, loved them" (Homily, Mass for the Possession of the Chair of St. Peter in Rome, Basilica of St. John Lateran, April 7, 2013).

This is the essence of God's mercy, the restoration of our state of grace through repentance and absolution. "What a beautiful truth of faith this is for our lives: the mercy of God!" the pope said in the same liturgy. "God's love for us is so great, so deep; it is an unfailing love, one which always takes us by the hand and supports us, lifts us up and leads us on."

We must trust in God, who cleanses us, renews us, and not only forgives but also forgets our sins, Pope Francis teaches us. Let us continually seek this grace.

Beauty of absolution

Jesus gave the Apostles the power to forgive sins. It is a little difficult to understand how a man can forgive sins, but Jesus gives this power. The Church is the depository of the power of the keys, of opening or closing to forgiveness. God forgives every man in his sovereign mercy, but he himself willed that those who belong to Christ and to the Church receive forgiveness by means of the ministers of the community. Through the apostolic ministry the mercy of God reaches me, my faults are forgiven and joy is bestowed on me. In this way Jesus calls us to live out reconciliation in the ecclesial, the community, dimension as well.

And this is very beautiful. The Church, who is holy and at the same time in need of penitence, accompanies us on the journey of conversion throughout our life. The Church is not mistress of the power of the keys, but a servant of the ministry of mercy and rejoices every time she can offer this divine gift.

General Audience
November 20, 2013

Joy of forgiveness

The joy of forgiveness is unmistakable, it radiates all around us whenever we experience it. Its source is God's love as he comes to meet us, breaking down the walls of selfishness that surround us and turning us into instruments of mercy.

Apostolic Letter
Misericordia et Misera, no. 3

The Church accompanies us

And we come to the second element: Jesus gave the Apostles the power to forgive sins. It is a little difficult to understand how a man can forgive sins, but Jesus gives this power.

The Church is the depository of the power of the keys, of opening or closing to forgiveness. God forgives every man in his sovereign mercy, but he himself willed that those who belong to Christ and to the Church receive forgiveness by means of the ministers of the community. Through the apostolic ministry the mercy of God reaches me, my faults are forgiven, and joy is bestowed on me. In this way Jesus calls us to live out reconciliation in the ecclesial, the community, dimension as well. And this is very beautiful.

The Church, who is holy and at the same time in need of penitence, accompanies us on the journey of conversion throughout our life. The Church is not mistress of the power of the keys, but a servant of the ministry of mercy and rejoices every time she can offer this divine gift.

General Audience of the Ministry of Mercy
November 20, 2013

Condemn sin, embrace the sinner

The Church condemns sin because it has to relay the truth: "This is a sin." But at the same time, it embraces the sinner who recognizes himself as such, it welcomes him, it speaks to him of the infinite mercy of God. Jesus forgave even those who crucified and scorned him.

The Name of God Is Mercy
Random House (2016), p. 50, Kindle Edition

Forgiveness with a caress

Jesus forgives. But there is something more here than forgiveness. For as a confessor Jesus goes beyond the law, for "the law said that [the woman caught in adultery] had to be punished" . . .

God doesn't forgive with a decree but with a caress. . . . caressing the wounds caused by our sins, because he is involved in forgiveness, is involved in our salvation. . . . God's mercy is great, God's mercy is great: forgiving us by caressing us.

Morning Meditation
April 7, 2014

Return to the source

We know that Jesus says that we should forgive seventy times seven: the important thing is to return frequently to the source of mercy and grace.

The Name of God Is Mercy
Random House (2016), p. 63, Kindle Edition

Not from our own efforts

First, the fact that the forgiveness of our sins is not something we can give ourselves. I cannot say: I forgive my
sins. Forgiveness is asked for, is asked of another, and in
Confession we ask for forgiveness from Jesus. Forgiveness
is not the fruit of our own efforts but rather a gift, it is a
gift of the Holy Spirit who fills us with the wellspring of
mercy and of grace that flows unceasingly from the open
heart of the Crucified and Risen Christ.

Secondly, it reminds us that we can truly be at peace
only if we allow ourselves to be reconciled, in the Lord
Jesus, with the Father and with the brethren. And we have
all felt this in our hearts, when we have gone to confession with a soul weighed down and with a little sadness;
and when we receive Jesus' forgiveness we feel at peace,
with that peace of soul which is so beautiful, and which
only Jesus can give, only Him.

General Audience
February 19, 2014

The Lord never tires of forgiving

The Lord never tires of forgiving: never! It is we who tire
of asking his forgiveness. Let us ask for the grace not to

tire of asking forgiveness, because he never tires of forgiving. Let us ask for this grace.

Angelus
March 17, 2013

Mercy triumphs over sin

Mercy will always be greater than any sin, no one can put a limit on the love of the all-forgiving God. Just by looking at him, just by raising our eyes from ourselves and our wounds, we leave an opening for the action of his grace. Jesus performs miracles with our sins, with what we are, with our nothingness, with our wretchedness.

The Name of God Is Mercy
Random House (2016), p. 86, Kindle Edition

Like branches to the vine

There are no difficulties, trials or misunderstandings to fear, provided we remain united to God as branches to the vine, provided we do not lose our friendship with him, provided we make ever more room for him in our lives. This is especially so whenever we feel poor, weak and sinful, because God grants strength to our weakness, riches to our poverty, conversion and forgiveness to our sinfulness. The Lord is so rich in mercy: every time, if we go to him, he forgives us. Let us trust in God's work!

The Lord is so rich in mercy: every time, if we go to him, he forgives us. Let us trust in God's work!

Homily
April 28, 2013

God forgives and forgets

Forgetting the past—this is God's weakness. When he embraces us, he forgives us, and forgets it. He doesn't remember. He forgets the past. When we sinners convert and let ourselves be re-encountered by God, reproach and sternness do not await us, because God saves, he welcomes us home again with joy and prepares a feast.

Angelus
September 11, 2016

"God's sickness"

When God forgives us, He forgets all the evil we've done. Someone has said "it's God's sickness." He doesn't have a memory. He can lose His memory in these cases. God loses his memory regarding the ugly story of so many sinners, of our sins. He forgives us and goes on. He only asks us to do the same: to learn to forgive, not to continue to bear this fruitless cross of hatred, of resentment, of "You're going to pay for this."

Morning Meditation
March 17, 2020

Don't stay down licking your wounds

It is different when someone relapses and commits the same sin and suffers because of it, when they have a hard time getting back on their feet. Many humble people confess to having fallen again. The most important thing in the life of every man and every woman is not that they should never fall along the way. The important thing is always to get back up, not to stay on the ground licking your wounds. The Lord of mercy always forgives me; he always offers me the possibility of starting over. He loves me for what I am, he wants to raise me up, and he extends his hand to me.

The Name of God Is Mercy
Random House (2016), p. 59-60, Kindle Edition

Starting over

It is important to be mindful of God's forgiveness, to remember his tender love, and taste again and again the peace and freedom we have experienced. For this is the heart of Confession: not the sins we declare, but the divine love we receive, of which we are ever in need. We may still have a doubt: "Confessing is useless, I am always committing the same sins." The Lord knows us, however; he knows that the interior struggle is difficult, that we are weak and inclined to fall, that we often relapse into doing what is wrong. So, he proposes that we begin to relapse into goodness, into asking for mercy. He will raise us up and make us new creatures. Let us start over, then, from Confession, let us restore to this sacrament the place it deserves in life and pastoral ministry!

Homily, Penitential Celebration
March 29, 2019

Lavishing grace

As St. Paul recalls: "in him we have redemption through his blood, the forgiveness of our trespasses, according to his grace which he lavished on us" (Eph 1:7-8). In this passage, "grace" is virtually synonymous with mercy, and we are told that God has "lavished" it upon us, meaning that it far exceeds our expectations, since it brings to fulfillment God's saving plan for each one of us.

General Audience
April 20, 2016

God is greater than our sin

Let us not forget this: God is greater than our sin! "Father, I do not know how to say it. I have committed many, serious [sins]!" . . . God is greater than all the sins we can commit. . . . His love is an ocean in which we can immerse ourselves without fear of being overcome: to God forgiving means giving us the certainty that he never abandons us. Whatever our heart may admonish us, he is still and always greater than everything (cf. 1 Jn 3:20), because God is greater than our sin.

General Audience
March 30, 2016

A new heart

This is how sinners are forgiven. They are not just comforted on the psychological level, because they are freed from the sense of guilt. Jesus does much more: he offers people who have made mistakes the hope of a new life. "But Lord, I am but a rag"—"Look forward and I will make you a new heart." This is the hope that Jesus gives us. A life marked by love.

General Audience
August 9, 2017

A new chance

Mercy is not opposed to justice but rather expresses God's way of reaching out to the sinner, offering him a new chance to look at himself, convert, and believe.

Misericordiae Vultus
Bull of Indiction of the Extraordinary Year of Mercy, no. 21

"Make me clean!"

Entrusting ourselves to God's will in fact means remitting ourselves to his infinite mercy. I will even share with you a personal confidence. In the evening, before going to bed, I say this short prayer: "Lord, if you will, you can make me clean!" And I pray five "Our Fathers," one for each of Jesus' wounds, because Jesus has cleansed us with his wounds. If I do this, you can do it too, in your home, and say: "Lord, if you will, you can make me clean!" and think about Jesus' wounds and say an "Our Father" for each of them. Jesus always hears us.

General Audience
June 22, 2016

The greatness of God

Let us keep this clearly in mind: Jesus is the Righteous One; he is not a sinner. But he wished to come down to us, sinners, and he prays with us, and when we pray, he is with us, praying; he is with us because he is in heaven, praying for us. Jesus always prays with his people, he always prays with us: always. We never pray alone; we always pray with Jesus. He does not stay on the opposite side of the river—"I am righteous, you are sinners"—to mark his difference and distance from the disobedient people, but rather he immerses his feet in the same purifying waters. He acts as if he were a sinner.

And this is the greatness of God, who sent his Son and annihilated himself, and appeared as a sinner. Jesus is not a distant God, and he cannot be so. Incarnation revealed him in a complete and humanly unthinkable way. Thus, inaugurating his mission, Jesus places himself at the forefront of a people of penitents, as if charging himself with opening a breach through which all of us, after him, must have the courage to pass. However, the road, the journey, is difficult; but he goes ahead, opening the way.

General Audience
October 28, 2020

Horizon of hope

God created us for joy and happiness and not to wallow in melancholic thoughts. This is why it is important to safeguard one's heart, defending ourselves from sad temptations that surely do not come from God. And whereas our strength appears weak and the battle against anxiety is particularly arduous, we can always turn to Jesus' name.

We can repeat that simple prayer, traces of which we also find in the Gospels and that has become the foundation of so many Christian spiritual traditions: A lovely prayer. "Lord Jesus Christ, Son of the living God, have mercy on me, a sinner!" This is a prayer of hope because I turn to Him, He who can open the doors wide and resolve the problem and have me look to the horizon, the horizon of hope.

General Audience
September 27, 2017

Burning bridges

It is not possible to adhere to Christ by placing conditions. It is necessary to detach oneself from certain bonds in order to truly embrace others. One is either well with God or well with the devil. For this reason, the renunciation and the act of faith go together. It is necessary to burn some bridges, leaving them behind, in order to undertake the new Way which is Christ.

General Audience
May 2, 2018

Weeping of repentance

Here we have to distinguish: there are those who become angry because they made a mistake. But this is pride. Instead, there are those who cry for the wrong done, for the good omitted, for the betrayal of the relationship with God. This is crying for not having loved, that springs from caring about the life of others. Here one cries because one does not match the Lord who loves us so much, and the thought of the good not done makes one sad. This is the sense of the sin. These people say: "I have hurt the one I love" and this causes them to suffer to the point of tears. May God be blessed if these tears arrive! This is the issue of one's errors that need to be faced, difficult but vital.

Let us think about the weeping of Saint Peter which takes him to a new and much truer love. It is weeping that purifies, renews. Peter looked at Jesus and cried: his heart had been renewed. Unlike Judas who would not accept that he had made a mistake and, poor wretch, killed himself. To understand sin is a gift from God, it is the work of the Holy Spirit. We cannot understand sin on our own. It is a grace that we have to ask. Lord may I understand the evil I have committed or might commit. This is a great gift and after understanding this, comes the weeping of repentance.

General Audience
February 12, 2020

Eight

Renewed in Grace

Pope Francis does not speak often of acts of penance following confession, but rather focuses on living out our interior conversion with the help of God's grace. Because we have been forgiven, we must forgive others; in fact, if we do not forgive others their offenses, we cannot receive forgiveness for our own, as we pray in the Our Father: "Forgive us our trespasses as we forgive those who trespass against us." And because we have been shown great mercy, we likewise are called to extend mercy to others. We too are sinners, and so we ought to exercise patience and understanding in dealing with our fellow sinners, hopefully leading them back to healing and wholeness in the Sacrament of Reconciliation as well.

A parable that Pope Francis uses to illustrate this truth is that of the merciful king and the wicked servant (Mt 18:21-35), in which the king forgives his penitent servant's considerable debt, after which the servant deals harshly with another servant who owes him a very small debt. When he heard of this outrage, the king had the wicked servant jailed.

"When we are tempted to close our heart to those who have offended us and tell us they are sorry, let us remember our Heavenly Father's words to the wicked servant: 'I forgave you all that debt because you besought me; and should not you have had mercy on your fellow servant, as I had mercy on you?' (Mt 18:32-33). Anyone who has experienced the joy, peace and inner freedom which come from being forgiven should open him or herself up to the possibility of forgiving in turn" (Angelus, St. Peter's Square, September 17, 2017).

Elsewhere, the pope often references the corporal and spiritual works of mercy as practical ways to respond to God's love and healing by showing mercy to others on our own.

The gift that keeps on giving

The mercy that we receive from the Father is not given as a private consolation, but makes us instruments that others too might receive the same gift. There is a wonderful interplay between mercy and mission. Experiencing mercy renders us missionaries of mercy, and to be missionaries allows us to grow ever more in the mercy of God. Therefore, let us take our Christian calling seriously and commit to live as believers, because only then can the Gospel touch a person's heart and open it to receive the grace of love, to receive this great, all-welcoming mercy of God.

Jubilee Audience
January 30, 2016

Meeting the "wounded"

The more conscious we are of our wretchedness and our sins, the more we experience the love and infinite mercy of God among us, and the more capable we are of looking upon the many "wounded" we meet along the way with acceptance and mercy.

The Name of God Is Mercy
Random House (2016), p. 67, Kindle Edition

Rejoice with repentance

So, we must avoid the attitude of someone who judges and condemns from the lofty heights of his own certainty, looking for the splinter in his brother's eye while remaining unaware of the beam in his own. Let us always remember that God rejoices more when one sinner returns to the fold than when ninety-nine righteous people have no need of repentance.

The Name of God Is Mercy
Random House (2016), p. 67-68, Kindle Edition

We must pardon others

Jesus affirms that mercy is not only an action of the Father, it becomes a criterion for ascertaining who his true children are. In short, we are called to show mercy because mercy has first been shown to us. Pardoning offenses becomes the clearest expression of merciful love, and for us Christians it is an imperative from which we cannot excuse ourselves.

At times how hard it seems to forgive! And yet pardon is the instrument placed into our fragile hands to attain serenity of heart. To let go of anger, wrath, violence, and revenge are necessary conditions to living joyfully.

Misericordiae Vultus
Bull of Indiction of the Extraordinary Year of Mercy, no. 9

Beauty of Confession

When one is in line to go to Confession, one feels all these things, even shame, but then when one finishes Confession one leaves free, grand, beautiful, forgiven, candid, happy. This is the beauty of Confession!

General Audience
February 19, 2014

Balm of grace

Ours is a heart conscious of having been created anew thanks to the coalescence of its own poverty and God's forgiveness; it is a "heart which has been shown mercy and shows mercy." It feels the balm of grace poured out upon its wounds and its sinfulness; it feels mercy assuaging its guilt, watering its aridity with love and rekindling its hope. When, with the same grace, it then forgives other sinners and treats them with compassion, this mercy takes root in good soil, where water does not drain off but sinks in and gives life. The best practitioners of this mercy that rights wrongs are those who know that they themselves have been shown mercy with regard to the same evil.

Second Meditation, Spiritual Retreat for the Jubilee of Priests
June 2, 2016

Forgive in order to be forgiven

We must forgive because God has forgiven us and always forgives us. If we do not forgive completely, we cannot expect to be forgiven completely. However, if our hearts are open to mercy, if we seal forgiveness with a brotherly embrace and secure the bonds of communion, we proclaim to the world that it is possible to overcome evil with good.

Angelus
February 24, 2019

Joyous heralds

If we think we don't need God who reaches out to us through Christ, because we believe we can make do on our own, we are headed for a fall. God alone can truly save and free us.

The Gospel is the real antidote to spiritual destitution: wherever we go, we are called as Christians to proclaim the liberating news that forgiveness for sins committed is possible, that God is greater than our sinfulness, that he freely loves us at all times and that we were made for communion and eternal life. The Lord asks us to be joyous heralds of this message of mercy and hope!

Message for Lent 2014

Forgive others with God's mercy

We have all heard this: "I can't forgive." But how can we ask God to forgive us if we are unable to forgive? Forgiving is something great, yet forgiving is not easy, because our heart is poor and with its efforts alone we cannot do it. However, if we open ourselves up to welcome God's mercy for ourselves, in turn we become capable of forgiveness.

General Audience
December 16, 2015

Conversion and generosity

If you want to know whether you are good Christians, you have to pray, try to draw near to Communion, to the Sacrament of Reconciliation. But the sign that your heart has converted is when conversion reaches the pocket, when it touches one's own interests. That is when one can see whether one is generous to others, if one helps the weakest, the poorest. When conversion achieves this, you are sure that it is a true conversion. If you stop at words, it is not a real conversion.

General Audience
August 21, 2019

Grace to improve

Faith in God asks us to renew every day the choice of good over evil, the choice of the truth rather than lies, the choice of love for our neighbor over selfishness. Those who convert to this choice, after having experienced sin, will find the first places in the Kingdom of heaven, where there is greater joy for a single sinner who converts than for ninety-nine righteous people (see Lk 15:7).

But conversion, changing the heart, is a process, a process that purifies us from moral encrustations. And at times it is a painful process because there is no path of holiness without some sacrifice and without a spiritual battle. Battling for good; battling so as not to fall into temptation; doing for our part what we can, to arrive at living in the peace and joy of the Beatitudes.

Today's Gospel passage calls into question the way of living a Christian life, which is not made up of dreams and beautiful aspirations, but of concrete commitments, in order to open ourselves ever more to God's will and to love for our brothers and sisters. But this, even the smallest concrete commitment, cannot be made without grace. Conversion is a grace we must always ask for: "Lord, give me the grace to improve. Give me the grace to be a good Christian."

Angelus
September 27, 2020

God puts us back on our feet

We all are sinners. We sinners, with forgiveness, become new creatures, filled by the spirit and full of joy. Now a new reality begins for us: a new heart, a new spirit, a new life. We, forgiven sinners, who have received divine grace, can even teach others to sin no more. "But Father, I am weak, I fall, I fall."—"If you fall, get up! Stand up!"

When a child falls, what does he do? He raises his hand to mom, to dad so they help him to get up.

Let us do the same! If out of weakness you fall into sin, raise your hand: the Lord will take it and help you get up. This is the dignity of God's forgiveness! The dignity that God's forgiveness gives us is that of lifting us up, putting us back on our feet, because he created men and woman to stand on their feet.

General Audience
March 30, 2016

Hope remains

This is one of the tasks of the Church: to help people perceive that there are no situations that they cannot get out of. For as long as we are alive it is always possible to start over, all we have to do is let Jesus embrace us and forgive us.

The Name of God Is Mercy
Random House (2016), p. 60, Kindle Edition

Witnesses to forgiveness

Dear brothers and sisters, God's forgiveness is what we all need, and it is the greatest sign of his mercy. It is a gift that every forgiven sinner is called to share with every brother and sister he meets. All those whom the Lord has placed beside us, family, friends, coworkers, parishioners . . . everyone needs, as we do, the mercy of God. It is beautiful to be forgiven, but you too, if you want to be forgiven, forgive in turn. Forgive! May the Lord allow us, through the intercession of Mary, Mother of Mercy, to be witnesses to his forgiveness, which purifies the heart and transforms life.

General Audience
March 30, 2016

"To forgive many things"

The Christian must forgive! Why? Because he has been forgiven. All of us who are here today, in the Square, we have been forgiven. There is not one of us who, in our own life, has had no need of God's forgiveness. And because we have been forgiven, we must forgive. We recite this every day in the Our Father: "Forgive us our sins; forgive us our trespasses as we forgive those who trespass against us." That is, to forgive offenses, to forgive many things, because we have been forgiven of many offenses, of many sins. In this way it is easy to forgive: if God has forgiven me, why do I not forgive others?

General Audience
September 21, 2016

The way of merciful love

Merciful love is therefore the only way forward. We all have a great need to be a bit more merciful, to not speak ill of others, to not judge, to not "sting" others with criticism, with envy and jealousy. We must forgive, be merciful, and live our lives with love.

General Audience
September 21, 2016

From the heart to the hands

Mercy, both in Jesus and in ourselves, is a journey which starts in the heart in order to reach the hands. What does this mean? Jesus looks at you, he heals you with his mercy, he says to you: "Arise!" and your heart is new. What does it mean to make a journey from the heart to the hands? It means that with a new heart, with the heart healed by Jesus I can perform works of mercy through the hands, seeking to help, to heal the many who are in need. Mercy is a journey that starts in the heart and ends in the hands, namely in the works of mercy.

General Audience
August 10, 2016

God's friendship

If you make a mistake, stand up again. There is nothing more human than making mistakes. And these same mistakes must not become a prison for you. Do not be trapped in your errors. The Son of God has come not for the healthy but for the sick; thus, he also came for you. And if you should err again in the future, do not be afraid; stand up again! Do you know why? Because God is your friend.

General Audience
September 20, 2017

A sign and instrument to others

He, in return, taught his disciples: "Be merciful, even as your Father is merciful" (Lk 6:36). It is a responsibility that challenges the conscience and actions of every Christian. In fact, it is not enough to experience God's mercy in one's life; whoever receives it must also become a sign and instrument for others. Mercy, therefore, is not only reserved for particular moments, but it embraces our entire daily existence.

General Audience
October 12, 2016

To live in charity

In the sacrament of forgiveness God shows us the way to turn back to him and invites us to experience his closeness anew. This pardon can be obtained by beginning, first of all, to live in charity. The Apostle Peter tells us this when he writes that "love covers a multitude of sins" (1 Pet 4:8). Only God forgives sins, but he asks that we be ready to forgive others even as he forgives us: "Forgive us our trespasses, as we forgive those who trespass against us" (Mt 6:12). How sad it is when our hearts are closed and unable to forgive! Resentment, anger and revenge gain the upper hand, making our lives miserable and blocking a joyful commitment to mercy.

Apostolic Letter
Misericordia et Misera, no. 8

Stake your lives on noble ideals

With him we can do great things; he will give us the joy of being his disciples, his witnesses. Commit yourselves to great ideals, to the most important things. We Christians were not chosen by the Lord for little things; push onwards toward the highest principles. Stake your lives on noble ideals, my dear young people!

Homily
April 28, 2013

A gesture, a word, a visit

Let us not fall into indifference, but become instruments of God's mercy. All of us can be instruments of God's mercy, and this will do more good to us than to others because mercy passes through a gesture, a word, a visit, and this mercy is an act of restoring the joy and dignity which has been lost.

General Audience
November 9, 2016

Compassionate sinners

Blessed are those who recognize their evil desires and who, with a contrite and humbled heart, stand before God and others not as righteous but as sinners. What Peter said to the Lord is beautiful: "Depart from me, Lord, for I am a sinful man." This is a beautiful prayer: "Depart from me, Lord, for I am a sinful man."

They are the ones who know how to have compassion, who know how to have mercy for others because they experience it themselves.

General Audience
November 21, 2018

We all can overcome with Christ's strength

It is tiring to fight against evil, to escape its deceit, to regain strength after an exhausting battle, but we must know that all of Christian life is a battle. We must also know, however, that we are not alone, that Mother Church prays so that her children, reborn in Baptism, do not succumb to the snares of the evil one but overcome them through the power of the Paschal Christ. Fortified by the Risen Christ who defeated the prince of this world (cf. Jn 12:31), we too can repeat with the faith of Saint Paul: "I can do all things in him who strengthens me" (Phil 4:13). We all can overcome, overcome anything, but with the strength that comes from Jesus.

General Audience
April 25, 2018

Sinners, but not corrupt

If a Christian truly allows himself to be cleansed by Christ, if he truly lets himself be stripped by Him of the "old man" in order to walk in a new life, although he remains a sinner—because we are all sinners—he can no longer be corrupted; the justification of Jesus saves us from corruption; we are sinners but not corrupt; one can no longer live with death in his soul, nor be a cause of death.

General Audience
March 28, 2018

The secret to mercy

Each person should remember that they need to forgive, they are in need of forgiveness and they need patience. This is the secret to mercy: by forgiving one is forgiven. Thus, God precedes us, and he forgives us first (cf. Rom 5:8). In receiving his forgiveness, we too are capable of forgiving. One's own misery and lack of justice therefore, become opportunities to open oneself up to the Kingdom of Heaven, to a greater measure, the measure of God who is mercy.

General Audience
March 18, 2020

Strength to go forward

From Jesus' forgiveness on the cross springs peace; true peace comes from the cross. It is the gift of the Risen One, a gift that Jesus gives us. Just think that the first greeting the Risen Jesus gives is "peace be with you," peace in your souls, in your hearts, in your lives. The Lord gives us peace; he gives us forgiveness, but we must ask: "deliver us from evil," in order not to succumb to evil. This is our hope, the strength given to us by the Risen One who is in our midst: he is here. He is here with that strength that he gives us to go forward, and he promises to deliver us from evil.

General Audience
May 15, 2019

"Lord, help me forgive"

If you do not forgive, God will not forgive you. Let us consider, we who are here, whether we forgive or whether we are able to forgive. "Father, I cannot do it, because those people treated me so harshly." But if you cannot do it, ask the Lord to give you the strength to do so: Lord, help me to forgive.

General Audience
April 24, 2019